Lee Bailey's

ONIONS

by Lee Bailey

Photographs by Tom Eckerle

*Recipe testing and development
with James Lartin*

CLARKSON POTTER/PUBLISHERS
NEW YORK

Published by Clarkson N. Potter/Publishers, 201 East 50th Street, New York, New York 10022. Member of the Crown Publishing Group.

Random House, Inc. New York, Toronto, London, Sydney, Auckland

CLARKSON N. POTTER, POTTER, and colophon are trademarks of Clarkson N. Potter, Inc.

Manufactured in China
Design by Howard Klein
Library of Congress Cataloging-in-Publication Data
Bailey, Lee.
[Onions]
Lee Bailey's onions / by Lee Bailey; photographs by Tom Eckerle; recipe testing and development with James Lartin.
          p.   cm.
1. Cookery (Onions) I. Title. II. Title: Onions.
TX803.05B35   1995
641.6'525—dc20
                                94-40097
                                CIP

ISBN 0-517-59748-9
10 9 8 7 6 5 4 3 2 1
First Edition

ACKNOWLEDGMENTS

James Lartin
Tom Eckerle
Barry Kornbluh
Tom Booth
in Tom's office, Meredith and Susan
Helen Skor
at Takashimaya, Lisa Bradkin

INTRODUCTION

You've all probably heard the old joke about the newlywed who asks her mother how to make an apple pie and is told, "Well, first you fry an onion."

"An onion?" she asks.

"Yes," says Mother, "to make the kitchen smell good."

Believe it or not, that got a pretty good laugh forty years ago. Today I'm not at all sure I could get away with it—and not just because it's an old chestnut. It's more likely that it wouldn't be considered ridiculous enough to seem funny.

To tell the truth, the more I got into this book and the more research I did, the more I came to appreciate how truly flexible and indispensable this homely vegetable really is. So, I certainly hope you see lots of things on the following pages to inspire you.

Cooked onions contribute a subtle, natural sweetness to dishes, and this sweetness intensifies as the onions brown and caramelize. Uncooked, they can add zing, crunch, or mellow sweetness, depending on which variety you opt for. And there *is* variety here. I've included several members of the onion's immediate family along with a couple of its relatives. There are yellow and white onions and their sweet cousins the Vidalias (or Walla Wallas or Mauis), but there are also sharp red onions, crisp green onions, and mild pearl onions. Leeks are here to add their mellow accent; garlic is scattered here and there, and I've even taken to garnishing some of these dishes with chives.

In many of the recipes that follow, onions act as the main flavoring ingredient, lending their characteristic magic to dishes as disparate as fritters, custards, breads, and soups. But in addition, there are recipes in which the onions themselves take center stage, as in my stuffed and baked onions or pickled onions. They also add their signature flavors to cooked and uncooked relishes, add zip and piquancy to salads—and certainly everybody knows what onions can do in a soup. These days, the idea of an onion and apple cobbler or an onion marmalade might not merit a raised eyebrow—but you never know. And the delicious watermelon and onion salad might just wake you up to a world of possibilities.

So the next time you see an onion, don't just think of making the kitchen smell good. Make something delicious. The world would be a poorer place without them.

Recipes

◆

You'll find that adding onions to your favorite breads and rolls can make a big difference. You could almost say it's a marriage made in heaven.

RED ONION FOCACCIA

◆

Try this basic onion focaccia as an accompaniment to soups and your favorite pasta dishes.

> *1 package active dry yeast*
> *½ teaspoon sugar*
> *1 cup lukewarm (105 to 115 degrees) water*
> *3 cups all-purpose flour*
> *1 teaspoon salt*
> *½ cup olive oil*
> *Kosher (coarse) salt*
> *6 to 8 small to medium red onions, halved,*
> *thinly sliced, and separated into pieces*
> *(about 3 cups)*

In a small bowl, combine the yeast, sugar, and lukewarm water. Set aside until foamy, 5 to 10 minutes.

Combine the flour and salt in a large bowl. Stir ¼ cup of the oil into the yeast mixture; add the liquids to the flour and stir to mix well. Add a bit more flour if the dough is too moist. Turn out the dough onto a lightly floured surface, and knead lightly until soft and elastic, 8 to 10 minutes.

Oil a large bowl and place the dough in it; oil the top of the dough. Cover and set aside in a warm, draft-free spot until doubled in size, about 45 minutes.

Punch down the dough and turn out onto a lightly floured surface. Pat out the dough into a large oval or rectangle about ½ inch thick; place on a lightly oiled baking sheet. Using your fingertips or bent knuckles, dimple the dough, forming small pockets over the entire surface. Pour on the remaining ¼ cup olive oil and spread out with the back of a spoon; sprinkle lightly with the salt. Cover the dough with the sliced onions.

Set the focaccia aside in a warm place to rise, uncovered, until almost doubled in bulk, 30 to 40 minutes.

Meanwhile, preheat the oven to 400 degrees.

Bake the focaccia until golden brown, about 30 minutes. Cool on a rack and serve at room temperature.

Serves 6

ONION CLOVERLEAF ROLLS

———◆———

I remember these cloverleaf rolls from when I was growing up.
I've updated them with onions.

> **4 cups diced onions**
> **¼ cup olive oil**
> **1½ teaspoons (½ package) active dry yeast**
> **1 teaspoon sugar**
> **¼ cup lukewarm (105 to 115 degrees) water**
> **2 tablespoons unsalted butter**
> **1 cup milk, scalded**
> **2 tablespoons instant mashed potato flakes**
> **3 cups bread flour**
> **1½ teaspoons salt**
> **White cornmeal**
> **Melted butter, for brushing the tops**

In a large skillet set over medium-high heat, sauté the onions in
the olive oil until golden brown, 10 to 12 minutes. Set aside to
cool to room temperature.

In a bowl, dissolve the yeast and sugar in the lukewarm
water. Stir well and set aside until frothy, 5 to 10 minutes.

Meanwhile, add the butter to the scalded milk and stir until
melted. Place the potato flakes into a small bowl, add the milk
and butter mixture, and stir to dissolve.

Combine the potato and yeast mixtures. Stir in the cooled
onions to incorporate.

In a large mixing bowl, stir together the flour and salt. Add
the potato-yeast-onion mixture and mix until the flour is moist-
ened. Using a mixer with a dough hook, knead the mixture until
it forms a ball and pulls away from the sides of the bowl, about
10 minutes.

Place the dough in a clean buttered bowl. Cover lightly and let rise in a warm, draft-free place until doubled in volume, about 1 hour.

Lightly butter a 12-cup muffin tin. Sprinkle each cup with a light coating of cornmeal; knock out any excess. Set aside.

Punch down the dough. Roll pieces of the dough into small, walnut-size balls; place 3 into each muffin cup. Brush the top of each roll with melted butter. Set aside in a warm place to rise until doubled, about 30 minutes.

Meanwhile, preheat the oven to 375 degrees.

Bake the rolls until golden, about 30 minutes. Turn out of the pan and serve hot.

Makes 12

***Onion Cloverleaf Rolls, Onion–Corn Muffins (page 14),
and slices of Red Onion Focaccia (page 10).***

ONION-CORN MUFFINS

———◆———

Here is my twist on old-fashioned corn muffins.

> **6 cups finely chopped onions**
> **8 tablespoons unsalted butter**
> **1 cup cornmeal**
> **⅔ cup all-purpose flour**
> **1 teaspoon baking powder**
> **1 teaspoon baking soda**
> **½ teaspoon salt**
> **2 eggs**
> **1½ cups low-fat sour cream**
> **¼ cup milk**

In a large skillet set over medium-high heat, cook the onions in 4 tablespoons butter until golden brown, 10 to 12 minutes.

Meanwhile, preheat the oven to 425 degrees. Line a 12-cup muffin tin with paper liners or butter the cups. Melt the remaining butter and let it cool to room temperature.

In a large bowl, whisk together the cornmeal, flour, baking powder, baking soda, and salt.

In another bowl, combine the eggs, melted butter, sour cream, and milk. Stir in the cooked onions. Add the onion mixture to the dry ingredients and fold together with a rubber spatula just until combined.

Fill each muffin cup three-fourths full of batter. Bake the muffins until golden brown, about 20 minutes. Cool them on a rack and serve them warm or at room temperature.

Makes 12

PIZZETTAS WITH HERB-ROASTED GARLIC

——◆——

Now this—a recipe that came from my friend Michael Chiarello—is a garlic-lover's dream.

> *1 tablespoon olive oil, plus additional as*
>   *needed*
> *2 teaspoons salt*
> *1 egg*
> *1 cup warm (110 to 115 degrees) water*
> *1 tablespoon dry active yeast*
> *3½ cups bread flour*
> *3 tablespoons chopped fresh rosemary leaves*
> *3 tablespoons freshly grated Parmesan cheese*
> *3 garlic cloves, minced*
> *3 Herb-Roasted Garlic bulbs (page 79)*

Combine 1 tablespoon oil with the salt, egg, and warm water in a large mixing bowl. Add the yeast and stir to dissolve. Add the flour and mix until the dough comes away from the bottom of the bowl; the dough will be slightly moist. Turn out onto a lightly floured surface and knead for 1 minute. Place the dough in an oiled bowl, oil the top of the dough, cover with a kitchen towel, and let rise in a warm place until doubled in bulk, 45 to 60 minutes.

Punch the dough down and cut into 3 equal pieces. Roll each piece into a ball, place on an oiled sheet, oil the dough, cover with a kitchen towel, and let rise again until doubled, 45 to 60 minutes.

Preheat the oven to 500 degrees. On a lightly floured surface, roll each ball out into an even circle, about 6 inches in diameter. Place on a baking sheet. Brush with olive oil and sprinkle each round with 1 tablespoon rosemary, 1 tablespoon

Parmesan, and 1 minced garlic clove. Bake for 5 minutes, then place one Herb-Roasted Garlic bulb in the center of each pizzetta. Return to the oven and bake for another 5 minutes or so, until golden brown.

Serve at once. As soon as it's cool enough to handle, pick up the garlic bulb and squeeze the pulp and juice over the pizzetta.

Makes 3

 **FRITTERS**

Fritters rhymes with *favorites—and that's what they are to me.
I grew up on all kinds, both fruit and savory. For those of you
who've never tried them, you're in for a surprise.*

GREEN ONION AND CORN FRITTERS

Serve these with barbecued meats and sausages. The trick
here is watchful frying. Make sure they're cooked through.

> *1 cup rice flour or all-purpose flour*
> *1 large egg white, beaten a few strokes with a*
>   *fork*
> *³/₄ cup water*
> *2 teaspoons* nuoc mam *(Vietnamese fish sauce;*
>   *see Note)*
> *1 tablespoon minced cilantro leaves and stems*
> *¹/₄ teaspoon curry powder*
> *1 teaspoon black pepper*
> *1¹/₂ cups fresh or frozen corn kernels*
> *3 large green onions, coarsely chopped with*
>   *some of the green*
> *Vegetable oil, for frying*

In a bowl, stir together the flour, egg white, water, and *nuoc mam*
until smooth. Stir in the cilantro, curry powder, and pepper, and
then fold in the corn and green onions.

Pour about ¼ inch of vegetable oil into a large skillet set over
medium heat. Heat until hot, but not smoking. Using a ¼-cup
dry measure as a scoop, spoon out portions of the batter and
ease them into the hot oil. Fry, without crowding the pan, until

the bottom of each fritter just begins to turn golden, about 1 minute. Turn and cook the other side until golden. Remove with tongs to drain on paper towels. Continue cooking fritters until all of the batter is used. Serve hot.

Makes about 18

Note: *Nuoc mam* is a fermented fish sauce available in the Oriental food section of many supermarkets or in specialty food stores.

ONION FRITTERS

◆

Another version of an old favorite.

> **1½ cups roughly chopped yellow onions**
> **½ cup roughly chopped shallots**
> **2 tablespoons olive oil**
> **3 green onions, finely chopped (use all of the green)**
> **⅔ cup all-purpose flour**
> **½ teaspoon salt**
> **⅛ teaspoon pepper**
> **1 egg yolk**
> **1 tablespoon unsalted butter, melted and cooled**
> **¾ cup flat beer**
> **1 egg white**
> **Vegetable oil, for frying**

In a large skillet set over medium-high heat, fry the onions and shallots in the olive oil until golden brown, 12 to 15 minutes. Stir in the green onions and sauté, stirring constantly, for 1 minute. Remove the pan from the heat and set aside to cool.

Meanwhile, combine the flour, salt, and pepper in a bowl; make a well in the center. In another bowl, whisk together the egg yolk, melted butter, and beer. Pour the liquids into the dry ingredients and blend until the batter is smooth and thick. Stir in the cooled onion mixture. Cover and allow the batter to rest for several hours, or cover and refrigerate overnight.

Just before frying beat the egg white until soft peaks form. Gently fold the white into the prepared batter; do not overmix.

In a deep-fryer, heat the oil to about 365 degrees. Working in batches, drop generous tablespoonfuls of the batter into the hot oil. Cook, turning gently, until dark golden brown all over and cooked through. Test the first fritter for doneness before going on; they can be deceptive, looking done on the outside while still raw in the middle. Drain the fritters on paper towels while you finish frying the batch. Serve hot.

Makes 24

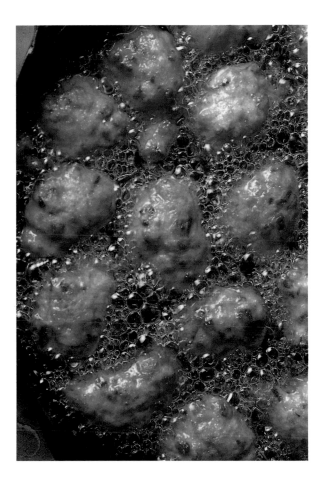

The soups in this group couldn't be more different but luckily are all delicious. As for the salads, we've all had onions in vinaigrette, but there may be a surprise in here for you.

ONION AND BLUE CHEESE CHOWDER

———◆———

The dash of Worcestershire sauce is a piquant addition here.

> **2 large Idaho potatoes, peeled and chopped**
> **4 cups chicken stock or broth**
> **1 bay leaf**
> **4 cups finely diced yellow onions**
> **2 tablespoons unsalted butter**
> **2 cups evaporated skim milk**
> **4 ounces blue cheese (Bleu d'Auvergne,**
> **Danablu, Maytag), crumbled**
> **1 teaspoon Worcestershire sauce**
> **1 tablespoon snipped fresh chives**

In a small saucepan, combine the potatoes, chicken stock, and bay leaf over medium-high heat. Cook until the potatoes are tender, 18 to 20 minutes.

Meanwhile, in a large, heavy saucepan set over medium heat, cook the onions in the butter, stirring occasionally, until very brown, about 15 to 18 minutes.

Remove the bay leaf from the potatoes. Puree the potatoes and stock. Add the milk and cheese and stir until melted.

Pour the pureed mixture into the pan of onions and stir well. Cook over medium-low heat until it is rewarmed and heated through, about 5 minutes. Be sure to scrape up any brown bits that are stuck to the bottom of the pot. Stir in the Worcestershire and garnish each serving of chowder with chives.

Serves 6

RICH ONION SOUP
———◆———

I like this very quick and easy soup in cold weather.

> **5¹/₂ cups finely chopped white onions**
> **¹/₃ cup finely chopped shallots**
> **4 tablespoons unsalted butter**
> **3 tablespoons all-purpose flour**
> **3 ¹/₂ cups chicken stock or broth**
> **¹/₂ cup heavy cream**
> **3 cups milk**
> **¹/₂ teaspoon salt**
> **¹/₂ teaspoon pepper**
> **Dash of grated nutmeg**
> **1 teaspoon Worcestershire sauce**
> **¹/₄ cup snipped fresh chives**

In a large saucepan set over low heat, cook the onions and shallots in the butter, stirring until wilted, about 15 minutes.

Sprinkle in the flour and cook, stirring constantly, for 3 minutes. Add the stock and stir well. Increase the heat to high and bring to a boil. Reduce the heat to medium, and cook until the soup begins to thicken.

Stir in the heavy cream, milk, salt, pepper, and nutmeg. Simmer over low heat to warm the milk and cream, about 5 minutes. Stir in the Worcestershire sauce.

Ladle the soup into bowls and garnish with chives.

Serves 6

SWEET ONION SOUP
WITH CHEESE CROUTONS

———◆———

My version of the classic.

> **5 cups thinly sliced yellow onions**
> **3 tablespoons unsalted butter**
> **4 cups chicken stock or broth**
> **$^1/_2$ teaspoon salt**
> **$^1/_4$ teaspoon pepper**
> **12 slices French bread ($^1/_4$ inch thick)**
> **Butter, for croutons**
> **Parmesan cheese, for croutons**

In a large stockpot set over medium heat, sauté the onions in the butter until very brown, about 30 minutes.

Stir in the chicken stock, salt, and pepper. Bring the soup to a boil over high heat. Reduce the heat to low, cover, and simmer for 45 minutes.

Meanwhile, make the croutons: Preheat the oven to 400 degrees.

Using a 1½-inch round cutter, cut out a round from each slice of bread. Butter both sides of each round and arrange on a baking sheet. Bake until both sides are golden brown, 6 to 8 minutes total. Remove the croutons from the oven, sprinkle with Parmesan cheese, and put back in the oven for the cheese to melt. Remove and allow to cool.

Top each serving of soup with 2 of the croutons.

Serves 6

VIDALIAS AND LEEKS VINAIGRETTE

———◆———

This combination, with its tomatoes and hard-cooked eggs, is almost a meal in itself.

> *2 large Vidalia or other sweet onions, trimmed*
> *and peeled*
> *3 leeks, trimmed to include 1½ inches of the*
> *light green, halved lengthwise, and washed*
> *well*
> *1 cup extra-virgin olive oil*
> *½ cup tarragon vinegar*
> *1½ tablespoons grated onion*
> *1½ tablespoons Dijon mustard*
> *1 teaspoon sugar*
> *Salt and pepper*
> *Lettuce leaves, for garnish*
> *1 cup peeled, seeded, and chopped ripe*
> *tomatoes*
> *2 hard-cooked eggs, pushed through a sieve or*
> *finely chopped*
> *½ cup finely chopped mixed fresh herbs*
> *(chervil, tarragon, parsley)*

Steam the sweet onions, covered, over boiling water until tender, about 20 minutes. Remove and set aside.

Steam the leeks over boiling water until tender, about 15 minutes. Remove and set aside.

In a large jar with a tight-fitting lid, combine the oil, vinegar, grated onion, mustard, sugar, and salt and pepper to taste. Cover and shake well to emulsify.

Line two salad plates with the lettuce. Quarter each onion. Split each leek half lengthwise. Divide the onions and leeks

between the plates. Garnish with the tomatoes and eggs. Shake
the dressing again and spoon some over each salad. Sprinkle
with the fresh herbs and serve.

Serves 2

LEEKS NIÇOISE

This is a pretty glamorous first-course salad by any measure.

> *¼ cup safflower oil*
> *¼ cup olive oil*
> *2 tablespoons minced garlic*
> *1 tablespoon dried thyme*
> *1 teaspoon black pepper*
> *6 large leeks, trimmed to include 2 to 3 inches*
>   *of the light green, halved lengthwise, and*
>   *washed well*
> *½ cup chicken stock or broth, heated*
> *½ pint cherry tomatoes, stemmed, washed, and*
>   *dried*
> *½ cup drained Niçoise olives*
> *1 teaspoon salt*

Combine the oils in a large skillet set over very low heat. Stir in the garlic, thyme, and pepper and heat for about 5 minutes to flavor and warm the oils and herbs without cooking them.

Add the leeks to the oil, tightly cover the pan, and simmer over low heat for 10 minutes. Turn the leeks with tongs and add the hot chicken stock. Cover again, increase the heat to medium, and simmer until the leeks are tender, 5 to 8 minutes. Remove the leeks to a serving dish.

Add the tomatoes, olives, and salt to the skillet and sauté over medium heat, shaking the pan gently to heat through without mashing the tomatoes, about 3 minutes.

Pour the mixture over the leeks. Serve at room temperature.
Serves 6

WATERMELON AND RED ONION SALAD
WITH RASPBERRY VINAIGRETTE

———◆———

This is my take on Jeremiah Tower's inventive creation.

> **2 cups cubed seeded watermelon**
> **½ red onion, thinly sliced**
> **2 tablespoons extra-virgin olive oil**
> **2 tablespoons raspberry vinegar**
> **½ cup fresh raspberries, crushed**
> **2 tablespoons sugar**
> **½ teaspoon salt**
> **¼ teaspoon pepper**
> **Boston lettuce leaves, for garnish**

In a large bowl, toss the watermelon with the red onion.

Make the raspberry vinaigrette: In a small jar with a tight-fitting lid, combine the oil, vinegar, raspberries, sugar, salt, and pepper. Cover and shake well.

Pour on the dressing and toss with the watermelon and red onion. Cover and refrigerate until very cold. Serve on chilled plates, garnished with the lettuce.

Serves 4

**ELISHES**

Here is a category with a few surprises and plenty of flavor. You'll find plenty of uses for them. Don't fail to try the marmalade, as unusual as it may seem to some of you.

ONION AND RAISIN RELISH

Onion and raisin relish is great with ham, pork loin, and other roasted meats.

> $^{1}/_{2}$ **cup golden raisins**
> $^{1}/_{3}$ **cup dried currants**
> **1$^{1}/_{4}$ pounds red or yellow onions, thickly sliced**
> **2 tablespoons unsalted butter**
> $^{3}/_{4}$ **cup chicken stock or broth**
> **1 teaspoon honey**
> $^{1}/_{2}$ **teaspoon finely chopped fresh or pickled**
> **jalapeño pepper**

Place the raisins and currants in a small bowl and cover them with hot water. Set aside.

In a heavy saucepan set over medium-high heat, sauté the onions in the butter, stirring occasionally, until just tender, about 7 minutes.

Reduce the heat to medium, add the chicken stock and honey, cover, and simmer until most of the liquid has been absorbed and the mixture has thickened slightly, about 10 minutes.

Drain the raisins and currants, and stir them into the mixture with the jalapeño. Cover and simmer for 5 minutes. Serve this cool or at room temperature.

Makes $^{3}/_{4}$ cup

ONION AND TOMATO RELISH

———◆———

Here is a fresh salsalike relish that is quick and easy.

> *1½ cups finely diced ripe tomatoes*
> *½ cup finely diced red onion*
> *½ cup finely diced Vidalia or other sweet onion*
> *¼ cup finely chopped green onions (use all of the green)*
> *¼ cup finely chopped shallots*
> *½ fresh or pickled jalapeño pepper, seeded and minced*
> *Juice of 1 small orange*
> *1 tablespoon balsamic vinegar*
> *2 tablespoons extra-virgin olive oil*
> *Salt and pepper*

Combine all of the chopped vegetables in a bowl.

In a jar with a tight-fitting lid, combine the orange juice, vinegar, oil, and salt and pepper to taste. Cover and shake well.

Pour the dressing over the vegetables and toss to coat. Set aside at room temperature for about 30 minutes before serving.

Makes about 2½ cups

RED ONION MARMALADE

◆

Here's the fabled red onion marmalade. This is one of those crossover foods. It can be served with meats—as it often is in the South—or with toast for breakfast.

> **4 tablespoons unsalted butter**
> **$1/2$ cup sugar**
> **$1^1/2$ pounds red onions, thinly sliced**
> **$2/3$ cup dry red wine**
> **$1/3$ cup plus 1 tablespoon white wine vinegar**
> **3 tablespoons crème de cassis liqueur**

In a nonreactive large saucepan set over low heat, melt the butter with the sugar until the sugar completely dissolves. Add the onions, cover, and cook until very soft, about 30 minutes.

Stir in the wine, vinegar, and cassis. Increase the heat to medium and bring to a boil. Lower the heat and simmer, uncovered, for 30 minutes. Increase the heat to high and boil, stirring constantly, until thick, about 5 minutes. Remove from the heat and set aside to cool to room temperature. Refrigerate in a covered container for up to 2 weeks.

Makes about 1 cup

PICKLED ONIONS

——◆——

I make these and just store them in the refrigerator because I am too lazy to go through the hassle of processing them; they will keep for a good while in the refrigerator, anyway.

> **8 cups small white pickling onions or pearl**
> **onions, peeled**
> **½ cup salt**
> **4 cups (1 quart) distilled white vinegar**
> **1 cup sugar**
> **2 tablespoons yellow mustard seeds**
> **1 tablespoon drained prepared horseradish**
> **20 white peppercorns**
> **4 bay leaves**
> **½ cup drained pimiento strips**

Sprinkle the onions with the salt. Cover with cold water and let stand for 6 to 8 hours or overnight. Rinse thoroughly with cold water, and drain well.

Combine the vinegar, sugar, mustard seeds, and horseradish in a nonreactive large saucepan and bring to a boil over high heat. Reduce the heat and simmer for 10 minutes.

Meanwhile, divide the onions among 4 clean pint-size jars. Add a few peppercorns, a bay leaf, and some of the pimiento to each jar. Pour the boiling hot vinegar mixture over the onions, leaving about ½ inch of head space at the top. Put the lids on, let cool, then refrigerate the jars for up to 2 weeks.

Makes 4 pints

OVERLEAF: *Onions in Seasoned Olive Oil (page 40)
and Onion and Celery Relish (page 41).*

ONIONS IN SEASONED OLIVE OIL

---◆---

Try this combination with your summertime sandwiches.

> *1 pound small white onions, peeled*
> *⅓ cup olive oil*
> *1 tablespoon honey*
> *2 tablespoons white wine vinegar*
> *¾ cup water*
> *½ teaspoon coriander seeds*
> *¼ teaspoon fennel seeds*
> *¼ teaspoon celery seeds*
> *6 shallots, sliced*
> *¼ teaspoon salt*
> *10 black peppercorns, crushed*
> *2 tablespoons chopped fresh parsley*

Place the onions in a nonreactive heavy saucepan and cover with all of the remaining ingredients except the parsley. Cover and cook over medium-high heat for 10 minutes.

Uncover the pan and cook for another 2 minutes or so, letting the onions brown slightly. Turn out into a serving dish and sprinkle with the parsley. Serve warm or at room temperature.

Makes 1½ cups

ONION AND CELERY RELISH

———◆———

This has crunch as well as flavor.

> **1 cup distilled white vinegar**
> **2 tablespoons confectioners' sugar**
> **2 tablespoons celery seeds**
> **2 cups thinly sliced small onions**
> **1 cup finely chopped celery**

In a bowl, stir together the vinegar and sugar until the sugar dissolves. Add the celery seeds, onions, and celery and mix well. Cover and refrigerate overnight. Serve very cold.

Makes 3 cups

REFRIGERATOR-WILTED ONIONS

———◆———

I've been dining on these since I was a child. Try them on sandwiches.

> **1 large yellow onion, thinly sliced (about**
> **2 cups)**
> **$^1/_2$ cup distilled white vinegar**
> **$^1/_2$ cup water**
> **1 cup oil**
> **$^1/_2$ teaspoon sugar**
> **$^1/_8$ teaspoon pepper**

Combine all of the ingredients in a deep glass or ceramic bowl. Stir to combine. Cover and refrigerate overnight.

Makes about 2$^1/_2$ cups

PASTA WITH SAUTÉED ONION SAUCE

My sautéed onion sauce is terrific as is, but it can also be thought of as a base for experimentation.

> *¹/₄ cup olive oil*
> *2 tablespoons unsalted butter*
> *2 pounds yellow onions, roughly chopped*
> *¹/₂ teaspoon salt*
> *¹/₄ teaspoon pepper*
> *1 pound dried fettuccine*
> *Shaved Parmesan cheese, for serving*

Combine the oil and butter in a large, heavy skillet over medium-high heat. Add the onions and sauté until golden brown, 10 to 12 minutes. Season with the salt and pepper.

Meanwhile, cook the pasta until al dente. Drain well.

Toss the cooked pasta with the sauce. Serve immediately, with the shaved cheese.

Serves 4

PENNE WITH ONIONS AND FENNEL

———◆———

The subtle flavor of fennel is a perfect complement to the sweet flavor of onions. Rosemary is a nice garnish here.

> **2 tablespoons unsalted butter**
> **¼ cup olive oil**
> **1 pound yellow onions, roughly chopped**
> **1½ pounds fennel bulb, trimmed and cut into**
> ** strips the size of the penne**
> **½ cup chicken stock or broth**
> **¼ teaspoon salt**
> **¼ teaspoon pepper**
> **1 pound dried penne**
> **Shaved Parmesan cheese, for serving**

Melt the butter with the olive oil in a large skillet over medium-high heat. Add the onions and sauté until lightly browned, 10 to 12 minutes.

Add the fennel to the onions and stir to combine. Stir in the chicken stock, salt, and pepper, and bring to a boil. Reduce the heat to medium-low, cover, and cook until the fennel is crisp-tender.

Meanwhile, cook the pasta until al dente. Drain well.

Toss the cooked pasta with the sauce. Serve immediately, with the Parmesan cheese.

Serves 4

OVERLEAF: *Pasta with Red Onion, Tomato, Basil, and Goat Cheese (page 48).*

PASTA WITH RED ONION, TOMATO, BASIL, AND GOAT CHEESE

———◆———

This is one of my all-time favorite summer pasta dishes.

> *1 pound dried fusilli*
> *¼ cup olive oil*
> *2 tablespoons butter*
> *1½ cups roughly chopped red onions*
> *1½ pounds ripe tomatoes, peeled, seeded, and*
> *   roughly chopped*
> *½ cup tightly packed shredded basil leaves*
> *4 ounces fresh goat cheese (chèvre), crumbled*
> *½ teaspoon salt*
> *¼ teaspoon pepper*

Cook the pasta until al dente.

Meanwhile, heat the oil and butter in a large skillet.

Drain the pasta. Add it to the skillet and toss with the hot butter and oil mixture; turn off the heat. Add the onions, tomatoes, and basil and toss to mix well. Add the cheese and toss to combine. Season with the salt and pepper. Serve at once.

Serves 4

PASTA WITH COOKED ONION, FRESH TOMATOES, AND FETA

————◆————

Here is a variation on my other summertime favorite.

> *1 pound dried pasta (any shape)*
> *½ cup olive oil*
> *2 tablespoons unsalted butter*
> *1½ pounds yellow onions, roughly chopped*
> *1 teaspoon salt*
> *¼ teaspoon pepper*
> *¼ teaspoon dried oregano*
> *1 pound ripe tomatoes, roughly chopped*
> *1 cup crumbled feta cheese*

Cook the pasta until al dente.

Meanwhile, heat the oil and butter in a large, heavy skillet set over medium-high heat. Add the onions and sauté until golden brown, 10 to 12 minutes. Season with the salt, pepper, and oregano.

Add the tomatoes to the skillet and cook over low heat, shaking the pan, just until the tomatoes are warmed through and have released some of their juices.

Drain the pasta and add to the sauce. Add the crumbled feta and toss to combine. Serve immediately.

Serves 4

SIDE DISHES

This category contains a lot of ideas for interesting side dishes—some of which may surprise you. At least I hope so.

CARAMELIZED ONIONS

————◆————

Make these to take along on a picnic or as an accompaniment to salads.

> *1½ pounds pearl onions or small white onions*
> *2 tablespoons unsalted butter*
> *2 tablespoons sugar*
> *1 cup water*
> *1 teaspoon balsamic vinegar*

Blanch the onions in rapidly boiling water for 15 to 20 seconds to loosen the skins. Drain and soak in cold water until cooled. Slice off the stem and root ends and peel. Cut an X in the root end of each onion to help prevent the onions from separating while they are cooking.

Combine 1 tablespoon of the butter, the sugar, and the water in a small saucepan. Add the onions and bring to a boil. Reduce the heat and simmer, uncovered, until the onions are tender and the liquid evaporates, about 15 minutes.

Add the remaining 1 tablespoon butter and the balsamic vinegar and stir to coat the onions.

Serves 4

PEPPERED THIN ONION RINGS

———◆———

You'll be pleased with how simple these are to make. The only problem is that you never seem to have quite enough of them.

> **3 medium onions**
> **Vegetable oil, for frying**
> **3/4 cup all-purpose flour**
> **1 tablespoon freshly ground black pepper**
> **Salt**

Cut off the stem end of each onion and peel. Slice very thin—you almost have to use a mandoline-type slicer to ensure even, thin slices. Separate the onions into rings.

Pour about 2 inches of oil into a deep-fryer or large sauté pan and heat to 365 degrees.

Meanwhile, combine the flour and pepper in a plastic bag. Add the onion rings and shake to coat; remove and shake off any excess flour.

Working in batches, drop some of the coated onions into the hot oil and fry very quickly until golden all over, about 2 minutes. Adjust the heat as necessary. Remove with a slotted spoon or tongs; drain on paper towels. Sprinkle with salt and serve hot.

Serves 6

BARBECUED ONIONS

As you can see, this little trick will work with any barbecue sauce.

2 pounds yellow onions, quartered
½ cup store-bought barbecue sauce

Preheat the oven to 400 degrees.

Break up the quartered onions into a mixing bowl. Add the barbecue sauce and mix to coat thoroughly. Scatter the coated onions over the bottom of a small roasting pan; cover with foil.

Roast for 10 minutes.

Remove the foil and roast until the onions are tender, 10 to 15 minutes longer.

Serves 6

INDIVIDUAL ONION CUSTARDS

———◆———

These little custards will enhance any composed salad or can be served as is. You can use mild or strong onions here.

> **6 thin slices day-old white bread**
> **2½ tablespoons unsalted butter**
> **1 pound onions, thinly sliced (about 3 cups)**
> **2 tablespoons chicken stock or broth**
> **1½ cups evaporated skim milk**
> **3 eggs or egg substitute**
> **½ teaspoon salt**
> **¼ teaspoon pepper**

Using a 3-inch round cookie cutter, cut one round from each piece of bread. Set aside, uncovered, to dry out.

Preheat the oven to 325 degrees. Lightly butter six 6-ounce ramekins or custard cups; set aside. Using 1 tablespoon of the butter, coat one side of the bread rounds.

Sauté the onions in the remaining 1½ tablespoons butter, stirring occasionally, until golden brown, 12 to 15 minutes. Add the chicken stock and cook, stirring to loosen anything stuck to the bottom of the pan. Remove the pan from the heat.

In a bowl, whisk together the milk, eggs, salt, and pepper. Evenly divide the cooked onions among the ramekins; pour in enough of the egg and milk mixture to fill each ramekin almost full. Top each ramekin with a bread round, buttered side up, and place in a low-sided baking dish. Fill the dish with hot water to come halfway up the sides of the ramekins.

Bake the custards until set, about 30 minutes.

Place under a hot broiler for several minutes until the bread is evenly browned. Serve hot.

Serves 6

ONION SOUFFLÉS

———◆———

You could also build a tasty little lunch around these individual soufflés. Just add a salad and a sorbet for dessert.

>*Softened butter and grated Parmesan cheese,*
>   *for the ramekins*
>*5 tablespoons unsalted butter*
>*3 tablespoons all-purpose flour*
>*1 cup milk, scalded*
>*2 cups finely diced onions*
>*3 egg yolks*
>*4 ounces sharp Cheddar cheese, grated (about*
>   *1 cup)*
>*2 ounces Emmentaler cheese, grated (about*
>   *½ cup)*
>*2 ounces Black Forest ham, very finely chopped*
>   *(about ½ cup)*
>*4 egg whites*

Lightly butter and sprinkle each of eight 6-ounce ramekins with Parmesan cheese; set aside. Preheat the oven to 350 degrees.

Melt 3 tablespoons of the butter in a small saucepan over low heat. Sprinkle on the flour and cook, stirring constantly, until an opaque paste forms and the flour is cooked, about 3 minutes. Gradually add the hot milk and cook, whisking constantly, until thickened. Set the white sauce aside to cool to lukewarm.

In a large skillet over medium heat, sauté the onions in the remaining 2 tablespoons butter, stirring occasionally, until golden brown, about 12 to 15 minutes.

Add the egg yolks, both grated cheeses, the ham, and the cooked onions to the cooled white sauce and mix well. Beat the egg whites to stiff, but not dry, peaks and gently fold into the cheese mixture. Divide the batter among the prepared ramekins.

Bake the soufflés until puffed and golden brown, 30 to 35 minutes. Remove from the oven and serve immediately.

Serves 8

CUBAN-STYLE STUFFED ONIONS

———◆———

These spicy stuffed onions make a delicious centerpiece for a luncheon or can be served as a first course.

6 medium white onions
2 tablespoons olive oil
½ pound ground beef
½ pound ground pork
1 16-ounce can Italian plum tomatoes, drained and chopped
1 4-ounce can mild green chilies, drained and chopped
¼ cup raisins
2 tablespoons tomato paste
2 garlic cloves, minced
1 tablespoon cider vinegar
¼ teaspoon ground cinnamon
⅛ teaspoon ground cloves
1 teaspoon salt
½ teaspoon pepper
½ cup coarsely chopped pimiento-stuffed olives
¼ cup coarsely chopped pimiento
2 cups beef stock or broth, boiling
Minced fresh parsley, for garnish

Peel the onions and remove ¼ inch of the stem end. Using a melon baller, scoop out the center of each onion, leaving a ¼-inch onion shell or cup. Finely chop the onion you removed and reserve 1 cup for the filling.

Blanch the onion shells in salted boiling water for 5 minutes. Remove from the water, rinse under cool water, and drain upside down on a wire rack until cooled to room temperature.

Preheat the oven to 350 degrees.

In a large, heavy skillet set over medium heat, sauté the reserved chopped onion in the olive oil until the onion is translucent, 3 to 4 minutes. Add the ground meats and cook, stirring occasionally, until they are no longer pink, 3 to 5 minutes. Stir in the tomatoes, green chilies, raisins, tomato paste, garlic, vinegar, cinnamon, cloves, salt, and pepper. Cook, stirring, until the excess liquid evaporates but the mixture is still moist, about 10 minutes. Stir in the olives and pimiento.

Sprinkle the drained onion shells with salt and pepper. Divide the stuffing equally among them, mounding the tops. Arrange the stuffed onions in a casserole or baking dish. Pour the hot stock around the onions into the bottom of the dish. Cover the dish with foil.

Bake for 45 minutes.

Serve hot, sprinkled with the parsley.

Serves 6

ONION POTATOES ANNA

———◆———

This is a variation of a classic I think you will find very pleasing. Use a good, sharp onion here.

> **2 pounds onions, thinly sliced**
> **4 tablespoons unsalted butter**
> **2 pounds (about 4 large) potatoes, peeled and**
>   **thinly sliced**
> **1 teaspoon salt**
> **¼ teaspoon pepper**

In a large skillet set over medium-high heat, sauté the onions in 3 tablespoons of the butter, stirring occasionally, until golden brown, 10 to 12 minutes.

Preheat the oven to 350 degrees.

Melt the remaining 1 tablespoon butter in a medium cast-iron skillet set over medium-high heat. Arrange a single layer of the potato slices in concentric circles, overlapping them slightly, over the bottom of the skillet. Sprinkle the potatoes with some of the salt and pepper. Spread one-third of the cooked onions on top of the potatoes. Repeat, layering the potatoes, salt and pepper, and onions until you have 3 layers of onions and 4 of potatoes.

Increase the heat to high and cook until the bottom layer of potatoes is golden brown, about 5 minutes. Check by picking up the edge of the potatoes with a metal spatula. When the bottom layer is browned, remove the skillet from the heat and tightly cover the pan with aluminum foil.

Bake until the potatoes are tender when stabbed with the tip of a sharp knife, about 45 minutes.

Remove the skillet to a wire rack, uncover, and let cool and set up slightly, 10 to 15 minutes.

Loosen the bottom of the potatoes with a spatula and by shaking the pan back and forth. Invert a serving dish over the skillet and flip the two together to unmold. Slice the potatoes and onions into 6 wedges and serve.

Serves 6

SAUTÉED ONIONS
WITH BALSAMIC VINEGAR

———◆———

Serve this with your favorite meat dish.

> **3 Spanish onions, thickly sliced**
> **¹/₄ cup olive oil**
> **2 tablespoons unsalted butter**
> **¹/₂ teaspoon salt**
> **¹/₄ teaspoon pepper**
> **¹/₄ cup balsamic vinegar**

In a large skillet set over medium-high heat, sauté the onions in the oil and butter, stirring occasionally, until golden brown, 10 to 12 minutes.

Season with the salt and pepper. Pour in the vinegar and stir to coat the onions. Cook for 1 minute. Serve hot or cool.

Serves 6

ROASTED WHOLE ONIONS
WITH BALSAMIC VINEGAR

———◆———

Guests love these very simple-to-do onions. And they don't take much doing.

> **6 small Vidalia or other sweet onions, peeled
>   and left whole
> 2 tablespoons olive oil
> 2 tablespoons balsamic vinegar
> 1/2 teaspoon salt
> 1/4 teaspoon pepper**

Preheat the oven to 350 degrees.

Quarter the onions lengthwise but leave them attached at the root ends. Place each onion on a small square of foil. Gently open each onion slightly and drizzle with some of the oil and then some of the balsamic vinegar, salt, and pepper. Wrap each onion in its foil and twist closed at the top.

Bake the onions until tender, 45 to 60 minutes.

Serves 6

These all make fine first courses. In a pinch you could build a light lunch around them.

LEEK TART

—◆—

While not a diet dish by any means, this is a slimmed-down version of the classic leek tart. Every little bit helps.

> *1½ cups all-purpose flour*
> *¼ teaspoon salt*
> *9 tablespoons (½ cup plus 1 tablespoon) cold*
> *   unsalted butter, cut up*
> *5 tablespoons ice water*
> *6 medium or 3 to 4 large (about 3 pounds) leeks*
> *½ cup chicken stock or broth*
> *4 ounces cured ham, such as Bayonne, finely*
> *   cubed (about ½ cup)*
> *2 ounces Gruyère cheese, grated (about ½ cup)*
> *1 egg*
> *½ cup evaporated skim milk*
> *¼ teaspoon salt (optional)*
> *½ teaspoon pepper*
> *Dash of grated nutmeg*

Make the pastry dough: In a food processor, combine the flour and salt and pulse once to mix. Add the butter and pulse until the mixture resembles coarse meal. Add the ice water and process just until the dough forms a ball; do not overwork the dough. Divide the dough into 2 pieces, one slightly larger than the other. Pat each into a disk and wrap in plastic. Chill for at least 30 minutes.

Meanwhile, preheat the oven to 400 degrees.

Make the filling: Trim the leeks and cut into 3-inch lengths. Split lengthwise and wash thoroughly several times in cold water. Cut the leeks into julienne.

In a large sauté pan with a tight-fitting lid, combine the leek julienne with the chicken stock. Cook over medium heat, stirring occasionally, until the leeks are tender and most of the liquid has been absorbed, 10 to 12 minutes. Remove from the pan and set aside to cool.

Meanwhile, roll out the larger piece of dough into a large circle. Fit the dough into a 9-inch tart pan with a removable bottom and trim off any overhang. Cover the dough with a sheet of foil and weigh down the foil with pie weights, dried beans, or rice. Blind-bake the crust for 10 minutes.

Remove the weights and foil, and bake the tart shell for 10 minutes longer. Remove from the oven and place on a wire rack.

Cover the bottom of the tart shell with the leeks. Scatter the ham and grated cheese over the top. In a bowl, combine the egg and evaporated skim milk. Add the salt, pepper, and nutmeg. Pour the mixture into the tart shell.

Roll out the remaining dough and cover the tart with it, crimping the edges. Cut several steam vents in the top of the dough.

Bake the tart until golden brown on top, 30 to 45 minutes.

Serves 6 to 8

OVERLEAF: *Leek Tart.*

YELLOW ONION TART

◆

This is creamier than the leek tart, but I bet you'll like them both.

1 1/2 cups all-purpose flour
6 tablespoons cold unsalted butter
2 tablespoons cold shortening
1/4 teaspoon salt
3 tablespoons ice water
4 tablespoons unsalted butter
1 pound yellow onions, very thinly sliced
1 bay leaf
1/2 teaspoon salt
1/4 teaspoon pepper
1 egg white, lightly beaten
3 eggs or egg substitute
1/2 cup milk
1/2 cup evaporated skim milk
Dash of grated nutmeg

Make the pastry dough: In a food processor, combine the flour, cold butter, shortening, and salt; pulse until the mixture resembles coarse meal. Add the ice water and process until the dough forms a ball. Pat the dough into a disk and wrap in plastic. Chill for at least 1 hour.

Meanwhile, in a large skillet, melt the butter over medium heat. Add the onions, bay leaf, salt, and pepper; cover and cook, stirring occasionally, until very dark brown, about 30 minutes. Remove from the heat and set aside.

Preheat the oven to 400 degrees.

Roll out the dough into a large round. Fit the dough into a 10-inch round fluted tart pan with a removable bottom; crimp the edges. Line the dough with foil and weigh down with pie weights, dried beans, or rice. Bake the tart shell for 10 minutes, until set.

Remove the weights and foil, and bake the shell for 10 minutes longer, until golden. Remove the shell from the oven and immediately brush it with the lightly beaten egg white. Return to the oven and bake for 1 minute. Remove and place on a wire rack. Reduce the oven temperature to 350 degrees.

In a bowl, whisk together the eggs, milk, evaporated skim milk, and nutmeg. Spread the onions into the tart shell. Pour the milk mixture over the onions.

Bake the tart until the filling is set, about 30 minutes.

Serves 6 to 8

CHEESE AND ONION PIE

◆

Don't be fooled by the simplicity of this wonderful dish. It's a winner.

> *1¼ cups all-purpose flour*
> *6 tablespoons cold unsalted butter*
> *2 tablespoons cold shortening*
> *¼ teaspoon salt*
> *3 tablespoons ice water*
> *2 pounds onions, thinly sliced*
> *¼ cup olive oil*
> *½ teaspoon dried thyme*
> *½ teaspoon dried oregano*
> *¼ teaspoon pepper*
> *½ cup chicken stock or broth*
> *6 ounces sharp Cheddar cheese, grated (about*
> *   1½ cups)*

Make the pastry dough: In a food processor, combine the flour, cold butter, shortening, and salt; pulse until the mixture resembles coarse meal. Add the ice water and process until the dough forms a ball. Pat the dough into a disk and wrap in plastic. Chill for at least 1 hour.

Meanwhile, in a large skillet set over medium-high heat, sauté the onions in the olive oil, stirring occasionally, until golden brown, 10 to 12 minutes.

Stir in the thyme, oregano, pepper, and chicken stock. Cook, stirring, until most of the stock evaporates. Remove from the heat and set aside.

Preheat the oven to 400 degrees.

Roll out the dough into a large round. Fit the dough into a 9-inch pie pan and crimp the edges. Line the dough with foil and weigh down with pie weights or dried beans. Bake the pie shell for 10 minutes.

Remove the weights and the foil and bake until golden brown, another 10 to 15 minutes. Remove and place on a rack. Spread the onions into the shell and sprinkle with the grated cheese. Bake until the cheese is bubbling and browned, about 15 to 20 minutes.

Serves 6 to 8

ONION AND APPLE COBBLER

◆

Don't be surprised by this combination. Just try it as an accompaniment to any spicy main course.

>*1½ cups all-purpose flour*
>*6 tablespoons cold unsalted butter*
>*2 tablespoons cold shortening*
>*¼ teaspoon salt*
>*3 tablespoons ice water*
>*1½ pounds onions, roughly chopped*
>*1½ pounds apples, peeled, cored, and roughly*
>*   chopped*
>*¼ cup packed light brown sugar*
>*¼ cup milk*
>*2 tablespoons unsalted butter*
>*1 tablespoon fresh lemon juice*
>*½ teaspoon salt*
>*Dash of cayenne pepper*

Make the pastry dough: In a food processor, combine the flour, cold butter, shortening, and salt. Pulse until the mixture resembles coarse meal. Add the water and process until the mixture starts to come together. Pat the dough into a disk and wrap in plastic. Chill for at least 1 hour.

Combine the onions, apples, brown sugar, milk, butter, lemon juice, salt, and cayenne in a large nonreactive saucepan set over medium-high heat. Bring to a boil. Reduce the heat to low, cover, and simmer until the apples are tender, about 10 minutes. Uncover, and cook until the mixture begins to thicken, about 5 minutes longer. Remove from the heat and set aside.

Preheat the oven to 400 degrees.

Roll out the dough into a large oval and line a 10-inch oval baking dish, leaving a 3- to 4-inch overhang around the sides of the dish. Spoon in the filling. Fold the edges of the dough up over the filling to cover most of it.

Bake until golden brown on top, about 30 minutes.

Serves 8

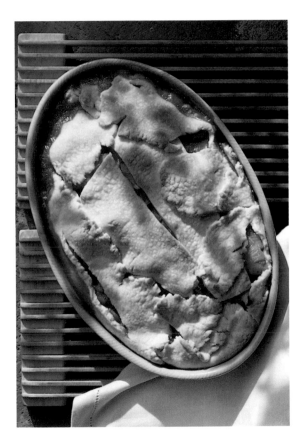

LASSICS

You've got one breakfast dish here and one main course. At one time or another, everyone has probably had at least one version of these dishes.

CLASSIC LIVER AND ONIONS

——◆——

I refer to this as classic liver and onions because it is just that—a classic.

> *1½ pounds yellow onions, thickly sliced*
> *6 tablespoons unsalted butter*
> *1 teaspoon sugar*
> *¾ cup water*
> *¾ teaspoon salt*
> *½ teaspoon pepper*
> *2¼ pounds calves liver*
> *All-purpose flour, for dredging*
> *3 tablespoons vegetable oil*
> *3 tablespoons Marsala wine*
> *1¼ cups beef stock or broth*

Place the onions, 3 tablespoons of the butter, the sugar, water, salt, and pepper in a small saucepan. Cover and bring to a boil over high heat. Reduce the heat to low, cover, and simmer for 2 minutes. Remove the lid and simmer, shaking occasionally, until the liquid is reduced and browned.

Wash the liver and dry with paper towels. Sprinkle lightly on both sides with salt and pepper. Place some flour into a plastic bag, add the liver, and shake to coat well. Remove the liver, shaking off any excess flour.

In a large, heavy skillet set over medium heat, melt the remaining 3 tablespoons butter with the oil until almost shimmering. Sauté the liver in batches, turning when browned on the outside and still pink on the inside, about 1½ minutes on each side. Remove to a platter and cover to keep warm until all of the liver is cooked.

Add the Marsala and stock to the pan, and cook over high heat, stirring up any browned bits from the bottom of the pan, until the sauce thickens, 2 to 3 minutes. Add the onions and stir to combine. Cover the liver with the sauce. Serve at once.

Serves 6

SCRAMBLED EGGS AND ONIONS

———◆———

Onions add zip to traditional scrambled eggs.

> **2 tablespoons unsalted butter**
> **$^1/_2$ cup finely chopped onion**
> **4 eggs, or 2 eggs plus 2 portions egg substitute**
> **1 tablespoon water**
> **$^1/_4$ teaspoon salt**
> **$^1/_8$ teaspoon pepper**

Melt the butter in a cast-iron or nonstick skillet set over medium-high heat. Add the onion and sauté, stirring occasionally, until golden brown, 8 to 10 minutes.

Meanwhile, beat the eggs with a whisk until light and fluffy. Add the water and whisk to combine.

When the onions are golden, pour the eggs in over them through a strainer. Reduce the heat to medium and scramble until cooked to your liking, usually 2 to 3 minutes. Sprinkle with the salt and pepper. Serve immediately.

Serves 2

ASICS

Here are two recipes that you should add to your repertoire.

SANTA FE ONIONS
◆

These onions can be made in batches and refrigerated. Add them to soups, sauces, even meat loaf. They are a welcome addition to most anything where you want to enhance the onion flavor.

2 large onions

Chop the onions coarsely by hand rather than with a food processor. They release too much juice if done in the machine.

Set a large cast-iron skillet over very high heat until very hot. Put enough onions into the pan to cover the bottom in a single layer. Cook, turning and stirring with a straight-edged, sharp metal spatula, until golden brown. Continue cooking, turning frequently, until caramelized to a very dark brown color. Remove from the pan and cook the remaining onions.

Place the onions in a plastic container and let cool to room temperature. Cover and store in the refrigerator.

Makes 1½ cups

HERB-ROASTED GARLIC

———◆———

You'll find countless uses for roasted garlic. Try it first spread on a piece of bread with a salad. Save the oil to use in vinaigrettes.

>*3 garlic bulbs (heads)*
>*1 cup olive oil*
>*1½ teaspoons minced fresh thyme*
>*1 tablespoon minced fresh rosemary*
>*Salt and pepper*

Preheat the oven to 350 degrees.

Cut off the tops of the garlic bulbs to expose the cloves. Brush generously with olive oil, then place in a small, ovenproof pan with the remaining oil. Sprinkle with the thyme and rosemary and season with salt and pepper. Roast for about 1 hour, until the garlic is tender and spreadable.

Makes 3 bulbs